S0-BDS-026

shooter

shooter

stimulating shots with a kick

Bath · New York · Singapore · Hong Kong · Cologne · Delhi · Melbourne

First published by Parragon in 2007

Parragon
Queen Street House
4 Queen Street
Bath BA1 1HE

Copyright © Parragon Books Ltd 2007

Designed by Talking Design
Photography by Mike Cooper
Introduction text and additional recipes by Linda Doeser
Food Styling by Lincoln Jefferson and Carole Handslip

All rights reserved. No part of this publication may be
reproduced, stored in a retrieval system, or transmitted
in any way or by any means, electronic, mechanical,
photocopying, recording, or otherwise, without the prior
permission of the copyright holder.

ISBN 978-1-4054-9511-0

Printed in China

WARNING
Recipes containing raw eggs are not suitable for convalescents, the
elderly, or pregnant women. Please consume alcohol responsibly.

CONTENTS

introduction

Often colourful, invariably tasty and with truly bizarre names, shooters are terrifically popular. Several servings can be made simultaneously as they are always served in small glasses. Making shooters isn't difficult and is great fun. Reading the following basic guidelines should guarantee you have all the skills of a professional bartender at your fingertips.

Bar Essentials

Cocktail shaker The standard type is a cylindrical 2¼-cup container with a double lid incorporating a strainer. The Boston shaker consists of double conical containers without a strainer.

Mixing glass You can use the container of your cocktail shaker, a pitcher about the same size, or a professional mixing glass.

Strainer A bar strainer prevents ice from being poured into the serving glass. You could also use a small nylon strainer.

Jigger This small measuring cup is often double-ended. A standard measure is 1½ oz (3 tbsp). Most jiggers have a 1½-oz cup one end and a ¾-oz cup the other. If you don't have a jigger, use a liqueur, schnapps, or shot glass.

Bar spoon This long-handled spoon is used for stirring cocktails in a mixing glass.

Other basics Lots of kitchen equipment is useful: corkscrew, citrus juicer, cutting board, measuring cups, and kitchen knives. You will require an ice bucket and tongs.

Glasses

Cocktail glass Stemmed glass with a cone-shaped bowl (4–5 oz)

Parfait glass Short-stemmed tube-shaped glass (1–2 oz)

Pousse-café glass Short-stemmed tulip-shaped glass (2 oz)

Shot glass Small glass (2 oz)

Bartender's Tips

Shaking cocktails Remove the lid from the shaker, add ice, and pour in the ingredients. Close and shake vigorously for 10–20 seconds, until the outside of the shaker is misty. Remove the small lid and pour the cocktail into the glass. If your shaker doesn't have an integral strainer, use a separate one.

Stirring cocktails Put ice into a mixing glass, pour in the ingredients, and stir vigorously for 20 seconds. Strain into a glass.

Layering pousse-café To make a multilayered drink, slowly pour the liqueurs or spirits over the back of a teaspoon into the glass. Each layer then settles on top of the layer before it.

Chilling glasses Place glasses in the refrigerator for 2 hours before using. Alternatively, fill them with cracked ice, stir well, then tip out the ice before pouring in the cocktail.

Ice To crack ice, put cubes in a strong plastic bag and hit with the smooth side of a meat bat or a rolling pin. Alternatively, bang the bag against a wall.

Party Starter

Tequila Slammer

SLAMMERS ARE A TYPE OF SHOOTER. THE IDEA IS THAT YOU POUR THE INGREDIENTS DIRECTLY INTO THE GLASS, WITHOUT STIRRING. COVER THE GLASS WITH ONE HAND TO PREVENT SPILLAGE, SLAM IT ON TO A TABLE TO MIX AND DRINK THE COCKTAIL DOWN IN ONE! DO ENSURE YOU USE A STRONG GLASS!

SERVES 1
1 measure white tequila, chilled
1 measure lemon juice
sparkling wine, chilled

1 Put the tequila and lemon juice into a chilled glass.
2 Top up with sparkling wine.
3 Cover the glass with your hand and slam.

Alabama Slammer

SMALL, BUT PERFECTLY PROPORTIONED—THIS IS A SHOOTER WITH A
REAL KICK!

SERVES 1
1 measure Southern Comfort
1 measure Amaretto
½ measure sloe gin
cracked ice
½ tsp lemon juice

1 Pour the Southern
  Comfort, Amaretto and
  sloe gin over cracked
  ice in a mixing glass
  and stir.
2 Strain into a shot glass
  and add ½ tsp lemon
  juice.
3 Cover and slam.

Brain Hemorrhage

THIS IS A RARE INSTANCE OF A COCKTAIL THAT IS DELIBERATELY INTENDED TO LOOK HORRID, RATHER THAN TEMPTING, AND WAS PROBABLY INVENTED TO DRINK ON HALLOWEEN.

SERVES 1
1 measure chilled peach schnapps
1 tsp chilled Baileys Irish Cream
½ tsp chilled grenadine

1 Pour the peach schnapps into a shot glass, then carefully float the Baileys on top. Finally, top with the grenadine.

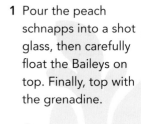

Firelighter

IF YOU ARE LOOKING FOR A COCKTAIL TO GIVE YOU A REAL KICK, THIS IS IT. THE INFAMOUS ABSINTHE IS A SERIOUSLY STRONG SPIRIT AND NOT TO BE TREATED LIGHTLY!

SERVES 1
1 measure absinthe, iced
1 measure lime juice cordial, iced

1 Ice a shot glass.
2 Shake the absinthe and lime over ice and, when well frosted, strain into the shot glass.

High Flyer

THESE TWO UNUSUAL LIQUEURS GIVE A VERY AROMATIC AND FRUITY COCKTAIL.

SERVES 1
⅔ measure gin
½ measure Strega
½ measure Van der Hum or
   Triple Sec
ice
orange or lemon peel

1 Stir the first three ingredients well over ice and strain into a tumbler.
2 Finish with a twist of peel.

Tornado

IF THESE LIQUORS ARE REALLY WELL ICED, YOU WILL CERTAINLY CREATE
A TORNADO IN YOUR GLASS WHEN YOU POUR ONE INTO THE OTHER—
JUST SIT AND WATCH THEM SWIRLING FOR A MOMENT!

SERVES 1

1 measure peach or other
favorite schnapps, frozen

1 measure black Sambuca,
frozen

1 Pour the peach
schnapps into an iced
shot glass.

2 Then gently pour on
the Sambuca over the
back of a spoon.

3 Leave it for a few
minutes to settle and
separate before you
down it.

Toffee Split

YOU SHOULD NOT NEED A DESSERT AS WELL, BUT YOU COULD ALWAYS POUR IT OVER SOME ICE CREAM.

SERVES 1
crushed ice
2 measures Drambuie
1 measure toffee liqueur,
  iced

1 Fill a small shot glass with crushed ice.
2 Pour on the Drambuie and pour in the toffee liqueur carefully from the side of the glass so it layers on top.
3 Drink immediately.

White Diamond Frappé

THIS IS A CRAZY COMBINATION OF LIQUEURS, BUT IT WORKS WELL ONCE YOU'VE ADDED THE LEMON. EXTRA CRUSHED ICE AT THE LAST MINUTE BRINGS OUT ALL THE SEPARATE FLAVORS.

SERVES 1
¼ measure peppermint schnapps
¼ measure white crème de cacao
¼ measure anise liqueur
¼ measure lemon juice
crushed ice

1 Shake all the liquid ingredients over ice until frosted.
2 Strain into a chilled shot glass and add a small spoonful of crushed ice.

XYZ

ICE COOL, THIS BEAUTIFULLY SIMPLE COCKTAIL IS VERY REFRESHING
AND MOREISH.

SERVES 1
½ measure fresh lemon juice
½ measure white rum
½ measure Cointreau
cracked ice
slice or twist of lime

1 Shake all the liquid
  ingredients together
  over ice until well
  frosted.
2 Strain into a chilled
  glass and dress with a
  slice or twist of lime.

Aurora Borealis

LIKE A POUSSE-CAFÉ, THIS SPECTACULAR COLORED DRINK SHOULD NOT BE MIXED OR STIRRED. LEAVE IT TO SWIRL AROUND THE GLASS, CREATING A MULTIHUED EFFECT AND TRY TO GUESS THE VARIOUS FLAVORS.

SERVES 1

1 measure iced grappa or vodka
1 measure iced green Chartreuse
½ measure iced orange Curaçao
few drops iced cassis

1 Pour the grappa slowly round one side of a well-chilled shot glass.
2 Gently pour the Chartreuse round the other side.
3 Pour the Curaçao gently into the middle and add a few drops of cassis just before serving. Don't stir. Drink slowly!

Cowboy

IN MOVIES, COWBOYS DRINK THEIR RYE STRAIGHT, OFTEN PULLING THE CORK OUT OF THE BOTTLE WITH THEIR TEETH, AND IT IS CERTAINLY DIFFICULT TO IMAGINE JOHN WAYNE OR CLINT EASTWOOD SIPPING DELICATELY FROM A CHILLED GLASS.

SERVES 1
3 measures rye whiskey
2 tbsp half and half cream
cracked ice cubes

1 Pour the whiskey and cream over ice and shake vigorously until well frosted.
2 Strain into a chilled glass.

Paradise

THIS FRUITY COMBINATION IS TRULY HEAVENLY WITH JUST A HINT OF
SHARPNESS TO PREVENT IT FROM BECOMING SICKLY SWEET.

SERVES 1
cracked ice
1 measure gin
½ measure apricot brandy
½ measure freshly squeezed
   orange juice
dash of lemon juice

1 Put the ice in a cocktail
shaker and pour in the
gin, apricot brandy,
orange juice, and
lemon juice. Close
the shaker and shake
vigorously for 10–20
seconds, until the
outside of the shaker
is misted. Strain into
a tumbler and drink
through a straw.

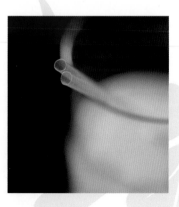

Sangrita

AS YOU NEED TO MIX THE INGREDIENTS AT LEAST AN HOUR IN ADVANCE, THIS IS THE PERFECT DRINK TO SERVE TO GUESTS AND CLOSE FRIENDS.

SERVES 16

2½ cups tomato juice
1¼ cups freshly squeezed orange juice
½ cup freshly squeezed lime juice
1 jalapeño chile pepper, seeded and finely chopped
1 tbsp Worcestershire sauce
1 tbsp Tabasco sauce
celery salt and ground white pepper
1 bottle (3¼ cups) tequila, chilled

1 Pour the tomato juice, orange juice, and lime juice into a large pitcher and stir in the chile, Worcestershire sauce, and Tabasco sauce. Season with celery salt and white pepper, then chill in the refrigerator for at least 1 hour, or longer if you want the mixture to taste spicier.

2 To serve, pour a measure of tequila into a shot glass and a measure of sangrita into a second shot glass. Drink the tequila in a single swallow, then chase with the sangrita.

Capucine

WELL-ICED LIQUEURS ARE OFTEN SERVED OVER FINELY CRUSHED ICE AS
A FRAPPÉ. THIS VERSION IS TIERED FOR TWICE THE EFFECT.

SERVES 1
crushed ice
1 measure iced blue Curaçao
1 measure iced Parfait
  Amour

1 Pack a small shot glass
  with finely crushed ice.
2 Pour in the Curaçao
  slowly and then
  carefully top up with
  the Parfait Amour.

Dandy

THE FRUIT FLAVOR ADDED AT THE END IS WHAT GIVES THIS RICH
COMBINATION A SPECIAL TOUCH.

SERVES 1
½ measure rye whiskey
½ measure Dubonnet
dash of Angostura bitters
3 dashes of cassis
ice
few frozen berries

1 Mix the first four
  ingredients with ice
  and strain into an iced
  shot glass.
2 Dress with a berry or
  two.

Layered Lift-Off

Pousse-Café

A POUSSE-CAFÉ IS A LAYERED COCKTAIL OF MANY DIFFERENT COLORED
LIQUEURS. IT IS CRUCIAL TO ICE ALL THE LIQUEURS FIRST.

SERVES 1
¼ measure grenadine
¼ measure crème de menthe
¼ measure Galliano
¼ measure kümmel
¼ measure brandy

1 Ice all the liqueurs and
   a tall shot or pousse-
   café glass.
2 Carefully pour the
   liqueurs over a spoon
   evenly into the glass.
3 Leave for a few
   minutes to settle.

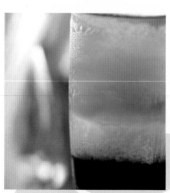

Angel's Delight

THIS IS A MODERN VERSION OF THE CLASSIC POUSSE-CAFÉ, AN UNMIXED, MIXED DRINK, IN THAT THE INGREDIENTS FORM SEPARATE LAYERS IN THE GLASS—PROVIDING YOU HAVE A STEADY HAND. YOU CAN DRINK IT AS A SLAMMER OR SIP IT.

SERVES 1
½ measure chilled grenadine
½ measure chilled Triple Sec
½ measure chilled sloe gin
½ measure chilled light cream

1 Pour the grenadine into a chilled shot glass or pousse-café glass, then, with a steady hand, pour in the Triple Sec to make a second layer.
2 Add the sloe gin to make a third layer and, finally, add the cream to float on top.

B-52

THE B-52 WAS CREATED IN THE FAMOUS ALICE'S RESTAURANT IN MALIBU, CALIFORNIA. THE NAME REFERS TO THE US B-52 STRATOFORTRESS LONG-RANGE BOMBER.

SERVES 1
1 measure chilled dark crème de cacao
1 measure chilled Baileys Irish Cream
1 measure chilled Grand Marnier

1 Pour the dark crème de cacao into a shot glass.
2 With a steady hand, gently pour in the chilled Baileys Irish Cream to make a second layer, then gently pour in the chilled Grand Marnier.
3 Cover and slam.

Nuclear Fallout

THIS IS SIMILAR TO A POUSSE-CAFÉ, WHERE THE LIQUEURS ARE
LAYERED, BUT, IN THIS CASE, THE HEAVIEST LIQUEUR IS COLDEST AND
ADDED LAST, TO CREATE THE SLOW DROPPING EFFECT!

SERVES 1
1 tsp raspberry syrup
¼ measure of maraschino
¼ measure of yellow
   Chartreuse
¼ measure Cointreau
½ measure well-iced blue
   Curaçao

1 Chill all the liqueurs but
  put the blue Curaçao in
  the coldest part of the
  freezer. Also chill a shot
  or pousse-café glass.
2 Carefully pour the
  drinks in layers over
  the back of a teaspoon
  except the blue
  Curaçao.
3 Finally, pour in the blue
  Curaçao and wait for
  the fallout!

Stars and Swirls

YOU WILL NEED A STEADY HAND FOR THIS ONE—PREFERABLY TWO PAIRS OF STEADY HANDS.

SERVES 1
1 measure Malibu
large ice cube
½ measure strawberry or
   raspberry liqueur
1 tsp blue Curaçao

1 Chill a small shot glass really well.
2 Pour in the Malibu and add a large ice cube.
3 Carefully pour in the other two liqueurs from opposite sides of the glass very slowly so they fall down the sides and swirl around.

Banana Bomber

THIS COCKTAIL IS AS DAZZLING AS IT IS DELICIOUS AND GLORIOUSLY ADDICTIVE. TRY IT WITH WHITE CRÈME DE CACAO AND A LAYER OF CREAM TOO—EQUALLY IRRESISTIBLE!

SERVES 1
1 measure banana liqueur
1 measure brandy

1 Pour the banana liqueur gently into a shot glass.
2 Gently pour in the brandy over the back of a teaspoon, taking care not to let the layers mix.

Fancy Free

THE KEY TO THIS LAYERED DRINK IS TO ICE THE LIQUEUR AND ICE THE
GLASS. IF IT DOES SEEM TO MIX ON IMPACT, GIVE IT A LITTLE TIME TO
SETTLE AND FORM ITS LAYERS AGAIN.

SERVES 1
⅓ measure cherry brandy,
   iced
⅓ measure Cointreau, iced
⅓ measure apricot liqueur,
   iced

1 Into an iced tall shot
glass pour the three
liqueurs in order. Pour
them over the back of
a spoon so they form
colored layers.

Fifth Avenue

AFTER-DINNER COCKTAILS OFTEN INCLUDE CREAM AND THIS ONE ALSO HAS THE DELICATE FLAVORS OF APRICOT AND COCOA.

SERVES 1

1 measure dark crème de cacao, iced

1 measure apricot brandy, iced

1 measure light cream

1 Pour the ingredients, one at a time, into a chilled glass. Pour the layers slowly over the back of a spoon resting against the edge of the glass. Each layer should float on top of the previous one.

African Mint

AMARULA IS A VERY RICH AND EXOTIC LIQUEUR, WHICH IS BEST SERVED AND DRUNK REALLY COLD—BUT NOT ON ICE AS THAT WILL DILUTE ITS REAL CHARACTER.

SERVES 1
¾ measure crème de menthe, chilled
¾ measure Amarula, chilled

1 Pour the crème de menthe into the base of a shot glass, saving a few drops.
2 Pour the Amarula slowly over the back of a spoon to create a layer over the mint.
3 Drizzle any remaining drops of mint over the creamy liqueur to finish.

Napoleon's Nightcap

INSTEAD OF HOT CHOCOLATE, HE FAVORED A CHOCOLATE-LACED BRANDY WITH A HINT OF BANANA AND MINT. DARING AND EXTRAVAGANT!

SERVES 1

1¼ measures cognac
1 measure dark crème de
  cacao
¼ measure crème de banane
ice
1 tbsp light cream

1 Stir the first three
   ingredients in a mixing
   glass with ice.
2 Strain into a chilled
   glass and spoon on a
   layer of cream.

After Five

ORIGINALLY THIS WAS THE NAME OF A MIXED COCKTAIL TOPPED
OFF WITH LEMONADE OR SODA. IT HAS NOW BEEN COMPLETELY
TRANSFORMED INTO A LAYERED SHOOTER WITH A REAL KICK.

SERVES 1
½ measure chilled
peppermint schnapps
1 measure chilled Kahlúa
1 tbsp chilled Baileys Irish
Cream

1 Pour the peppermint
schnapps into a shot
glass. Carefully pour
the Kahlúa over the
back of a teaspoon so
that it forms a separate
layer. Finally, float the
Baileys Irish Cream on
top.

The Perfect Shot

Sputnik

IF YOU ARE MAKING SEVERAL OF THESE THEY CAN BE PREPARED IN
ADVANCE WITH DIFFERENT COLORED CHERRIES IN ORBIT ON TOP.

SERVES 1
1 measure vodka
1 measure light cream
1 tsp maraschino
ice
maraschino cherry

1 Shake all the liquid
   ingredients well over
   ice and strain into a
   glass.
2 Finish with a cherry
   supported on 2 or
   more crossed cocktail
   sticks.

Perfect Love

THIS IS THE LITERAL TRANSLATION FOR AN UNUSUAL PURPLE LIQUEUR
FLAVORED WITH ROSE PETALS, ALMONDS, AND VANILLA.

SERVES 1
1 measure vodka
½ measure Parfait Amour
½ measure maraschino
scoop crushed ice

1 Shake all the liquid
ingredients together
over ice until frosted.
2 Strain into a chilled
shot glass with more
ice.

Depth Charge

ANISE IS A PARTICULARLY UNUSUAL DRINK IN THAT IT TURNS CLOUDY WHEN MIXED WITH WATER BUT NOT WHEN MIXED WITH OTHER ALCOHOLIC DRINKS, UNTIL THE ICE STARTS MELTING. SO DRINK IT SLOWLY, WITH CARE, AND WATCH IT CHANGE.

SERVES 1
1 measure gin
1 measure Lillet
2 dashes Pernod
ice

1 Shake all the liquid ingredients over ice until well frosted.
2 Strain into a shot glass.

Peach Floyd

SHOTS LOOK STUNNING IN THE RIGHT TYPE OF GLASS, BUT AS THEY
ARE FOR DRINKING DOWN IN ONE, KEEP THEM SMALL AND HAVE
EVERYTHING REALLY WELL CHILLED.

SERVES 1
1 measure peach schnapps,
  chilled
1 measure vodka, chilled
1 measure white cranberry
  and peach juice, chilled
1 measure cranberry juice,
  chilled
ice

1 Stir all the liquid
  ingredients together
  over ice and pour into
  an iced shot glass.

Jealousy

THIS REALLY IS AN AFTER-DINNER COCKTAIL AND IF YOU WANT A
CHANGE, YOU COULD OCCASIONALLY FLAVOR THE CREAM WITH A
DIFFERENT LIQUEUR.

SERVES 1
1 tsp crème de menthe
1–2 tbsp heavy cream
2 measures coffee or
    chocolate liqueur
chocolate matchsticks

1 Gently beat the mint
   liqueur into the cream
   until thick.
2 Pour the coffee liqueur
   into a very small iced
   glass and carefully
   spoon on the whipped
   flavored cream.
3 Serve with chocolate
   matchsticks.

Tequila Shot

ACCORDING TO CUSTOM THIS IS THE ONLY WAY TO DRINK NEAT TEQUILA. IT IS OFTEN DESCRIBED AS BEING SMOOTH AND TART, SO ADDING LIME JUICE AND SALT MAY SOUND CONTRADICTORY, BUT IT WORKS!

SERVES 1
1 measure gold tequila
pinch of salt
wedge of lime

1 Pour the tequila into a shot glass.
2 Put the salt at the base of your thumb, between thumb and forefinger.
3 Hold the lime wedge in the same hand.
4 Hold the shot in the other hand.
5 Lick the salt, down the tequila and suck the lime.

Alaska

YELLOW CHARTREUSE IS SLIGHTLY SWEETER THAN GREEN CHARTREUSE, SO IT DOES BENEFIT FROM BEING REALLY WELL CHILLED.

SERVES 1
½ measure gin
½ measure yellow
   Chartreuse
ice

1 Shake the liquid
   ingredients over ice
   until well frosted.
2 Strain into a chilled
   glass.

Breakfast

IT IS DIFFICULT TO BELIEVE THAT ANYONE WOULD ACTUALLY HAVE THE STOMACH TO COPE WITH COCKTAILS FIRST THING IN THE MORNING— BUT THEN, FOR THOSE WHO PARTY ALL NIGHT AND SLEEP ALL DAY, COCKTAIL TIME COINCIDES WITH BREAKFAST.

SERVES 1
2 measures gin
1 measure grenadine
cracked ice cubes
1 egg yolk

1 Pour the gin and grenadine over ice in a shaker and add the egg yolk.
2 Shake vigorously until frosted. Strain into a chilled glass.

Voodoo

THIS ENTHRALLING MIXTURE OF FLAVORS IS GUARANTEED TO WEAVE A SPELL ON YOUR TASTE BUDS AND WORK ITS MAGIC FROM THE VERY FIRST SIP.

SERVES 1
½ measure chilled Kahlúa
½ measure chilled Malibu
½ measure chilled
    butterscotch schnapps
1 measure chilled milk

1 Pour the Kahlúa, Malibu, schnapps, and milk into a glass and stir well. Drink through a straw.

Whiskey Sour Jelly Shot

A NEW TWIST ON A CLASSIC COCKTAIL FOR A NEW GENERATION OF COCKTAIL DRINKERS, BUT BE CAREFUL TO KEEP CHILDREN AWAY FROM THE REFRIGERATOR.

SERVES 8
1 packet lemon Jello
½ cup hot water
¾–1 cup bourbon whiskey

1 Break up the Jello and place it in a large heatproof measuring cup or pitcher. Pour in the hot water and stir until the Jello has dissolved. Let cool, then stir in the whiskey to make the mixture up to 2 cups.

2 Divide among 8 shot glasses and chill in the refrigerator until set. Once set remove from the refrigerator and eat with a spoon.

Margarita Jelly Shot

IT IS NOT ESSENTIAL TO FROST THE GLASSES WITH SALT BUT IT DOES
LOOK ATTRACTIVE AND PAYS HOMAGE TO THE ORIGINAL NON-JELLY
COCKTAIL RECIPE OF 1942.

SERVES 8
½ lime, cut into wedges
2 tbsp fine salt
1 packet lime Jello
1 cup hot water
4 tbsp Cointreau
scant 1 cup tequila

1 Rub the outside rims
   of 8 shot glasses with
   the lime wedges, then
   dip in the salt to frost
   them. Set aside.
2 Break up the Jello
   and place it in a large
   heatproof measuring
   cup or pitcher. Pour
   in the hot water and
   stir until the Jello
   has dissolved. Let
   cool, then stir in the
   Cointreau and tequila
   to make the mixture
   up to 2 cups. Divide
   among the prepared
   shot glasses, taking
   care not to disturb the
   salt frosting, and chill
   in the refrigerator until
   set.

Peppermint Patty

SOMETIMES THE SIMPLE THINGS IN LIFE ARE THE BEST AND THIS PERFECT COMBINATION OF CHOCOLATE AND PEPPERMINT IS JUST SUCH A ONE.

SERVES 1
cracked ice
1 measure white crème de cacao
1 measure white crème de menthe

1 Put the ice in a cocktail shaker and pour in the crème de cacao and crème de menthe. Close the shaker and shake vigorously for 10–20 seconds, until the outside of the shaker is misted. Strain into a shot glass.

Prairie Oyster

FOR TIMES WHEN YOU REALLY CAN'T LIFT YOUR HEAD OFF THE PILLOW, IT'S THE ONLY THING TO TRY.

SERVES 1
Worcestershire sauce
vinegar
tomato ketchup
1 egg yolk
cayenne pepper

1 Mix equal quantities of Worcestershire sauce, vinegar and ketchup and pour into a chilled glass.
2 Add the yolk carefully without breaking.
3 Do not stir, sprinkle with cayenne pepper and down it all in one!

Hair of the Dog

THIS WELL-KNOWN EXPRESSION—A DROP OF WHATEVER GAVE YOU THE HANGOVER—IS IN FACT A POPULAR SCOTTISH "MORNING AFTER" TIPPLE!

SERVES 1
1 measure bourbon whiskey
1½ measures half and half
  cream
½ measure clear honey
ice

1 Gently mix the whiskey, cream and honey together.
2 Pour into a shot glass over ice and serve.

Zipper

THIS SHOOTER GETS ITS NAME FROM AN UNUSUAL, NOT TO SAY
"LOUCHE METHOD" OF SERVING IT, BUT TASTES JUST AS GOOD SERVED
MORE CONVENTIONALLY.

SERVES 1
crushed ice
1 measure tequila
½ measure Grand Marnier
½ measure light cream

1 Put the crushed ice
into a cocktail shaker
and pour in the tequila,
Grand Marnier, and
cream. Close the
shaker and shake
vigorously for 10–20
seconds, until the
outside of the shaker
is misted. Strain into a
shot glass.

index